The Nativi COLOR & CUT OUT
ACTIVITY BOOK

Illustrated by Mary Rojas

warner press
KiDs

305800214226

Helpful Hints:

1. Color the Bible characters and then cut out, using the dotted line as a guide. If copies are made, use index paper or thicker paper, so the characters are sturdy enough to stand.

2. Cut out the stands and match up with the appropriate characters. (The matching stand might not be on the same page as the character.)

3. Fold the stands along the dotted lines. See Figure A.

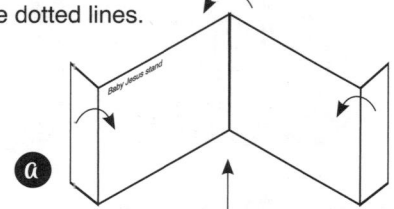

4. Attach stands to the back of the characters using tape following the general placement seen in Figure B below.

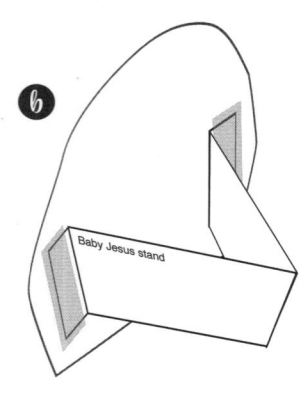

Position the stand close to the sides and towards the lower half of the character. Use tape to cover the tabs so it is secure. The stand should angle down slightly so that when it is standing, it is tilting back. The stand fold should not go lower then the base. Adjust if necessary.

5. Attach the star to the tip of a pipe cleaner or straw. Then tape to the back of the stable in the shaded area. The lower you can tape the pipe cleaner, the more sturdy the stable should be. See Figure C.

6. Attach the stand to the back of the stable.

   Or for a sturdier stable, use an empty cereal or cracker box. First cover with black or dark blue paper, then glue or tape the stable to the front bottom edge and adhere star in the sky. See Figure D. The rest of the cut-outs can be placed inside the box for easy transport and storage. (You will need to make a copy of "The Nativity Story" and place on the back side of the box.)

7. Read "The Nativity Story" on the back of the stable while you act out the story with the Bible characters. Share with your family and friends!

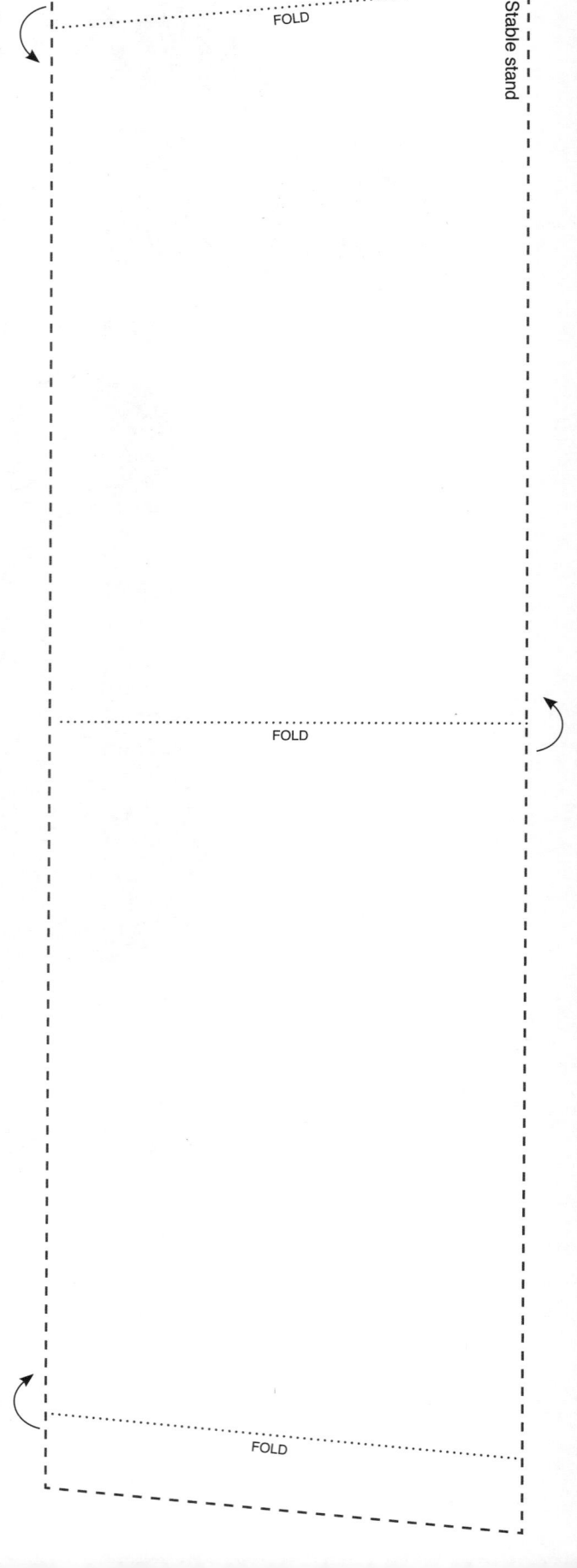

FOLD

FOLD

FOLD

Stable stand

The Nativity Story

God chose Mary and Joseph to be the parents of His Son. Then Mary and Joseph had to go to Bethlehem. Jesus was born there, in a stable where animals lived. Mary put Jesus in a manger to sleep.

In a field near Bethlehem, shepherds were watching their sheep at night. Angels came and told the shepherds some good news.
"Jesus is born!" they said.

Later, wise men followed a star to find Jesus. The wise men gave Jesus special gifts. Then they worshiped Jesus, God's gift to the world!

For unto you is born this day…a Saviour, which is Christ the Lord.

LUKE 2:11

Pipe Cleaner placement

Mary and Joseph stand

FOLD
FOLD
FOLD

Baby Jesus stand

FOLD
FOLD
FOLD

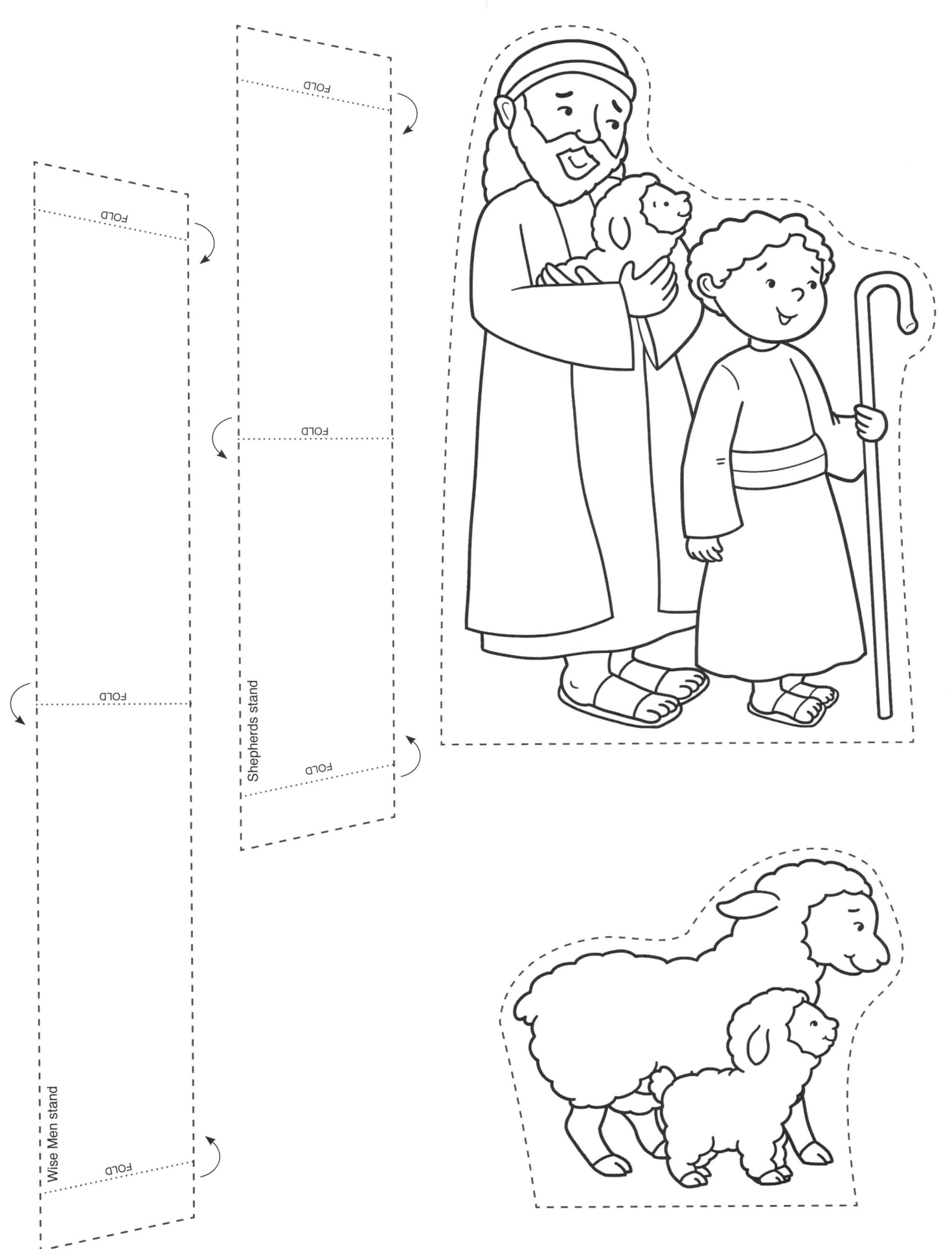

Shepherds stand

Wise Men stand

Sheep stand

FOLD   FOLD   FOLD

Camels stand

FOLD

FOLD

FOLD

Angel stand

FOLD · FOLD · FOLD

Angel stand

FOLD · FOLD · FOLD

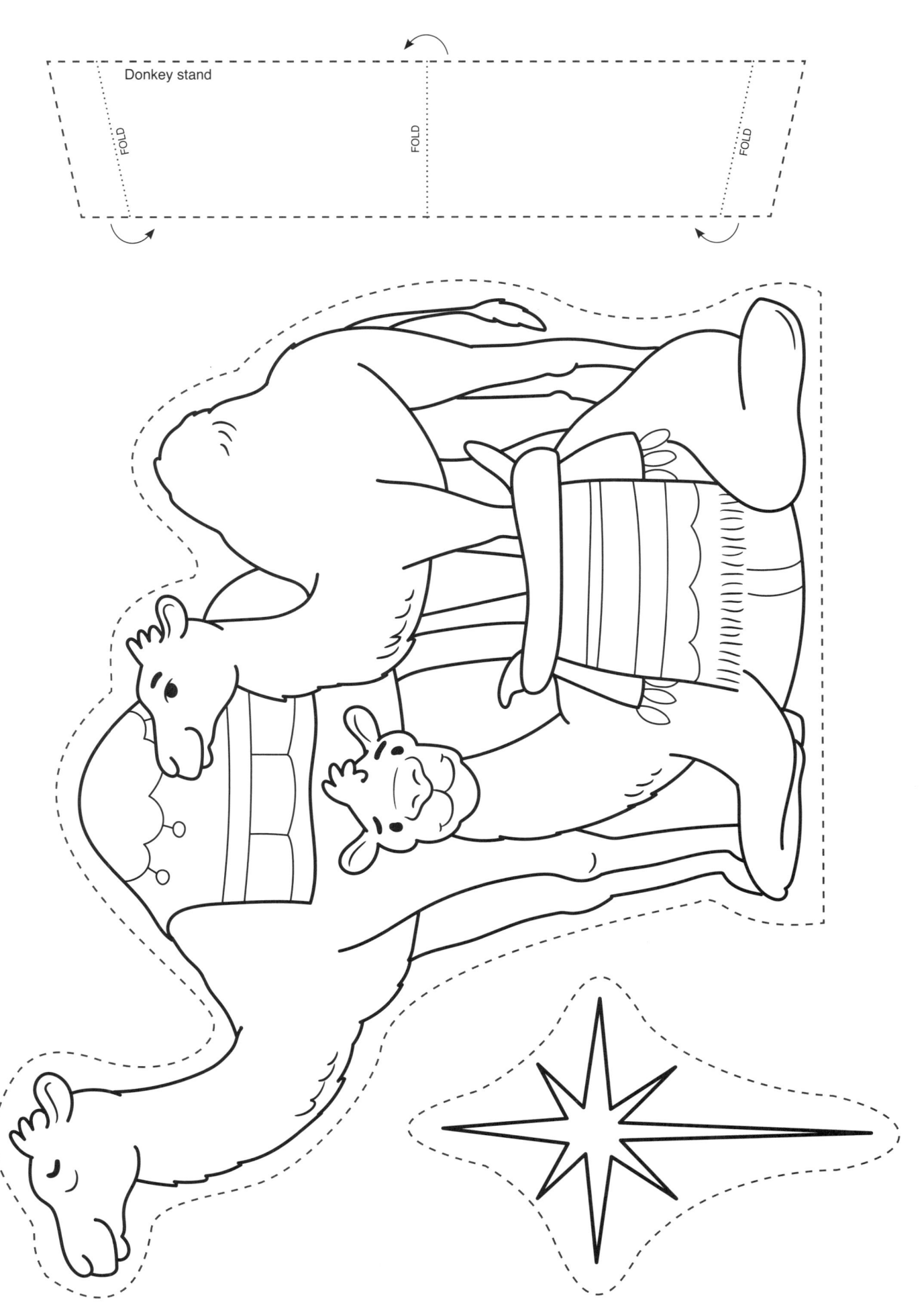

Donkey stand

FOLD

FOLD

FOLD